HER 20 SomeTHINGS

A Young Woman's Guide To Navigating Through Her Prime

Zakiyrah Ficklin

Foreword by Octavia Samuels

Copyright © 2016 by Zakiyrah Ficklin
Edited by: Jasmine Spratt
Cover Photography: Jonquille Arnold
Ordering information:
Special discounts are available on quantity purchases by organization, corporation and others.
For details contact:
Her20somethings@gmail.com
www.her20somethings.com

All rights reserved. No parts of this work may be reproduced, or transmitted in any form or by any mean, electronic or mechanical, including, photocopying, or by any information storage or retrieval system, except as is explicitly permitted by the Copyright Act or in writing from the author.

www.zakiyrahficklin.com

Dedication

I dedicate this book to all of my Queens in their 20-somethings. May God continue to bless you and guide you!

Special Thank You to Carlas (CJ) Quinney President, Eric Thomas and Associates LLC.

CJ was the inspiration for this book…I can remember sitting at CJ's desk during one of my dad's sessions and talking to him about my book idea. CJ crushed my whole idea! He changed my perspective on things. He said that I needed to max out the level that I was at in life and reach out to young women in my age range. At that moment… Her 20 SomeTHINGS was born.

Table of Contents

Foreword..6
Introduction...8
Her Relationships 18
Her Spiritual Walk..................................23
Her Mother's Womb...............................28
Daddy's Girl...34
Her Gift..39
What's Holding Her Back........................43
Who is She?..59
Traits of Extraordinary Women...............62
How To Find Purpose............................71
Finding Your Balance With Life..............78
Living Up To Others Expectations.........89
Spending Money Wisely........................94
Learn New Things................................100
Blaming The Past.................................104
Know Your Limits.................................107
Strengths and Weaknesses..................112
Personal Core Values...........................117
Traveling is Worth The Investment........122
Adopt a Mentor.....................................126

Build Muscle of Self-control……………………..130
Believe You Can Do It…..……………………….134
Setting and Executing Goals…………………..138
It's Okay To Ask For Help……………………...145
Life is About Experiences……………………...148
Failure is Unavoidable…………………………153
Ask For What You Want………………………....156
Extracting Networks……………………………158
Relationships…………………………….....……162
"Things I Know Now"……………………….…..164

Foreword

When I decided to become a mentor to a young girl, I didn't know that I would start a profitable business, author a book and build a youth focused non-profit. I never fathomed that the young girl would become my intern and we would conquer the world together. Over the years our relationship has blossomed into a friendship and sisterhood. Zakiyrah Ficklin is my shero! She took the hand she was dealt, built fulfilling relationships, gives back to young girls as founder of H.E.R. Foundation and does it all with a fashionable flare! Zakiyrah is the epitome of feminism and a hero that believes in her God given destiny.

The journey of life is interesting, in that while you think you're teaching, you really are learning. I've learned the greatest life lessons from Zakiyrah. She always listens, works hard, chooses the smart option and considers the feelings of others.

I am great because I met a young girl named Zakiyrah, she said yes to greatness and believed in purpose. As you read Her 20 SomeTHINGS you have a divine opportunity to choose your own greatness and live your purpose on purpose. Zakiyrah authored a book that allows you to transition from pain to purpose! You will find that through your obstacles, you've been equipped with every essential gift needed to continue toward your destiny. As I learned from Zakiyrah, I encourage you to listen to the words of wisdom in HER 20 SomeTHINGS and let them guide you to your next level.

You only need to believe and say, "YES", to greatness. In the stories of others we can recognize ourselves and choose to be amazing! I celebrate you for choosing to read HER 20 SomeTHINGS. I know that in you we all win and together we get to conquer the world.

-Minister Octavia Samuels

Introduction

It was a hot, summer day in Dallas, but the way she felt made her days feel and look so gloomy. She rolled out of her comfy king-size bed and started to the kitchen. She began her daily routine. She filled her favorite teapot from Teavanna with raspberry and peach tea. She couldn't live a day without drinking her favorite teas. As the water boiled on the stove, she plopped down on the couch and turned on her recordings of *Fix My Life* by Iyanla Vanzant. "What if I could get on this show and Iyanla could fix my life?" She thought to herself sarcastically.

Monica was a 24-year-old woman with a Bachelor's degree in communications. She worked as a marketing and branding manager for a small media company in Dallas, Texas. She was the middle child of three and had a great relationship with her parents. However, Monica's relationship with her dad wasn't always great. She disliked him for such a long time up until her late teens. She hated and blamed him for her parents getting a divorce. She felt like he callously left their family - and that they weren't a priority to him anymore. He would lie to her on several occasions. She would often feel like the little girl after school, sitting on the steps, waiting for her daddy to come and get her, yet daddy never showed up. She blamed him for the trust issues she had with men. Monica hated making her issues everyone else's issue, so as a child she kept everything bottled in and never desired to talk about anything.

    Despite all of the emotional distress with her father, Monica had a great relationship with her siblings as they were growing up. But one day her little brother decided he wanted to live the street life. It took a major toll on their immediate family. As a result, their family outings soon came to an end, and Monica began to feel like she had lost one of her best friends. As a young girl, she mainly struggled with the reality of her broken family. She wanted a family with both of her parents and her siblings together as one. After her parents divorced, Monica thought she would never see that again. Through her grade school years, she met several people because she went to many different schools. She attended two elementary schools, three middle schools, and two high schools. She hated her last year of high school. It was her first year at a new school, she did not know anyone, and she was not trying to get to know anyone. She did not participate in any extracurricular activities, and she did not even want to go to her prom. During Monica's last year of high school, she went through a tough time that was devastating for her. Her best friend's brother molested her at the age of 17. She couldn't believe in a million years that this would be something that she would have to go through. Abashed, ashamed, angry, and depressed were some of the emotions that Monica felt. She did not want to talk to anyone regarding the situation. For an entire month, she cried herself to sleep. She jumped every time someone touched her, and she lived each day in fear of someone else sexually taking advantage of her.

The affect of the molestation led to a pregnancy. She did not know how to feel at this point. She did not want to keep a child that was conceived wrongfully, as this child would be a constant reminder of what happened to her. After talking to her family about the pregnancy, Monica decided to have an abortion. After the abortion, she thought that she would hate herself forever.

The loud, whistling noise grew louder and louder and suddenly, Monica jumped off the couch to turn the stove off. The loud noise was coming from the teapot that Monica had seemingly forgotten about. She grabbed her Chanel tea-mug out of the cabinet and filled it with raspberry and peach tea.

"Ring, ring, ring" Monica could hear the loud vibrations from her cell phone that was in her bedroom, as she stood in the kitchen. She ran to the room to catch her phone. "Hey babe, what are you doing?" said the voice on the other end of the phone. It was her boyfriend. "Just drinking some tea and watching some recordings... coming over?" Monica smiled and said. "Yep, be there in 5," her boyfriend said.

"Knock, knock, knock" Monica heard as she hurriedly ran to answer the door. She swung the door open and to her surprise, Isaiah was standing there holding a dozen red roses. She gave him a big hug. "Good to see you," she said, as they both walked in the house. She closed the door and locked it back. They went to the kitchen and Monica asked Isaiah if he was hungry. "As a lion," Isaiah said. Monica opens the refrigerator and pulls out a half of cantaloupe, turkey bacon, and eggs. As she cooked Isaiah breakfast, he stood there admiring her beauty. With no makeup on, just sweatpants, and a t-shirt - Monica felt more beautiful than ever. As Isaiah stood there watching Monica, he asked her a question. "Are you happy with me?" Monica slowly turned her head to him and said, "Yes babe." All the while, in her head, she was thinking of how lonely she felt. She gave him a slight smile then she started back preparing breakfast. Isaiah smiled back, went in the living room, and turned the television to ESPN.

"Babe, your food is ready," Monica yelled. Isaiah walked back into the kitchen and sat down at the kitchen table. Monica grabbed her raspberry and peach tea in her Chanel mug and joined Isaiah at the table. As they sat at the table eating breakfast, Monica began to talk to him about some of the goals that she had in mind. She told him she wanted to write a book, start a non-profit organization, purchase a home, and start traveling out of the country more. She also told him that she wanted to relocate. She shared that she was tired of Dallas and wanted to explore a new city. Isaiah sat quietly as he listened to everything Monica had to say. Finally, he responded and said, "Why would you move? You're fine here. Where will you get the money to fund a book? You don't get paid to own a non-profit. Where will you get the money to travel?" Monica looked at him and agreed, "you're right," she said.

Deep down Monica resented the fact that she was so in love with this man and yet he didn't support her vision for her life. After they finished breakfast, Monica picked the dishes up from the table and hand washed them in the sink. She pulled out a drying towel and laid it across the counter. She sat the dishes on the towel for them to dry. Isaiah was running late for his basketball game, so he kissed Monica's forehead, and told her he would call her later as he headed out the door.

It was 2:53 a.m. and Monica found herself sitting, all alone, on the bathroom floor crying her heart out. She was beginning to hate the feeling of fear, pain, agony, and heartbreak. She had a job that overworked her, friends who were already successful, self-defeating feelings of not being good enough, and a boyfriend who didn't support her. Monica went through each day trying to please everyone else but herself. She put so much good into the world and did not see much good in return. Her inner self felt like she should be more successful than she was at this very moment. She had so many goals but could not conquer any of them because of the defeat she held in her mind. She wanted to see the finished product of success for her life, but did not want to go through the process to get to the product. In Monica's mind, she was behind in life because many of the people that she grew up with were already accomplishing greater things than her.

She found herself giving up a lot, and starting things but not finishing them. She was hurting – mentally, spiritually, and emotionally. Monica didn't have a clue how she would escape this dark place that she'd hid in over the last couple of years of her life. She felt stagnated in every area of her life. Monica began to drift away into deep thought and all of her dreams and aspirations began to overpower her fears.

It get's exhausting trying to "keep it together", to keep saying that you're fine when you're really not, and to suffer in silence because you feel it's your only option. There will always be problems in your life, but sometimes we don't have the capacity to handle them all by ourselves. Give your pain a voice, and let someone listen. You will be amazed at how much weight will be lifted off your shoulders. Instead of suffering in silence like Monica, get help with any situation that feels unbearable or any scar that feels unhealable.

Part One

Her

Her Relationships

"To share your weakness is to make yourself vulnerable; to make yourself vulnerable is to show your strength."
~Criss Jami~

Relationships are about learning, growing, and connecting – beginning with the relationship we have with ourselves. Relationships are not something that we just know. We learn them. While growing up, besides the physical lessons – we learn language so that we can communicate our needs and begin to understand the needs of others. We learn love and how to connect, which is essential in successfully developing relationships with others.

Somewhere along the lines, we disconnect and as a result, it stunts our growth.

Monica's inability to grow beyond what she had experienced in her relationships – with her parents, siblings, significant other, and self was the cause of her spiritual, mental, and emotional hurt.

A lot of times we think that we have these great relationships, but sometimes they are extremely surface. We have to learn to go deeper with our relationships and become intimate (into-me-see), which means being vulnerable and open and allowing others to see your heart for what it truly is.

An example of a surface relationship:

The relationship with a mother and daughter can be surface when there are no real problems, but the daughter does not feel comfortable talking about certain topics with her mother, or answering questions like "how was your day?" with a "good, great, or okay."

An example of a deeper relationship:

The relationship with that same mother and daughter could go deeper when that daughter begins to start high school, her body begins changing, she's into boys, and thinking about having sex. Her ability to be comfortable and go have a conversation with her mother about these things let's us know they have a connection and deeper relationship.

Are your relationships the cause of your hurt?

_____

_____

_____

Describe your current relationships with:

Mother:

_____

_____

_____

_____

_____

Father:

_____

_____

_____

_____

_____

_____

_____

Significant other:

_____
_____
_____
_____
_____
_____
_____
_____

Self:

_____
_____
_____
_____

** Challenge**

I challenge you to identify a relationship that has been surface and go deeper.

SN: If you don't get your expected results, KEEP TRYING!

Her Spiritual Walk

"Our heavenly Father understands our disappointment, suffering, pain, fear, and doubt. He is always there to encourage our hearts and help us understand that He's sufficient for all of our needs."

~Charles Stanley~

Monica always longed to have a close, intimate relationship with God, similar to that of a best friend who you can talk to about anything, laugh with, pray with, and grow with throughout life. She would go to church every Sunday and pray everyday, but she still felt a void and no sense of closeness to God.

One day she was extremely down. It was raining; she had a massive headache, at that moment, she didn't really see any reason to smile; she battled with self-issues, stress, depression, self-esteem, and fear. Monica felt a void of not having anyone close and she just wanted someone to love her unconditionally. She wanted that close bond with her parents, siblings, friends, and that special person. She didn't like to burden people with her problems, so she would keep them all to herself. When her mind became too full to hold anything else, she would get to a breaking point and it would erupt like a volcano. She had so many people around her, yet Monica still felt alone. One day she went into her closet and sat on the floor and cried aloud. She cried for hours and then, suddenly, she sat up and began talking to God about how she felt. She knew her parents loved her, she knew her siblings loved her, she knew her friends loved her, but she still felt a void of love and loneliness. She yearned for a man to love her, but God said to her loud and clear "Monica, they love you but I deliberately placed this void in your heart because it can only be filled with me, I need you to trust me." " I need you to surrender your heart to me."

Have you ever been in a room full of people, but still felt alone? There are times when God takes you through seasons of isolation so that you can understand what he is trying to tell you or get you to understand. God uses those seasons of isolation to bring us closer to Him, strip us of what is not needed, and shape us into what we need to become. The reward of being isolated is much greater than the suffering period. It is hard but it is in that moment, you realize that you are not truly alone and it does not last forever.

When was the last time you had to trust God?

_____

_____

_____

_____

_____

_____

_____

_____

_____

_____

What was the outcome?

_____

_____

_____

_____

_____

What did you learn from the outcome?

_____
_____
_____
_____
_____
_____
_____
_____
_____
_____

What are you going through right now where it requires trusting God?

_____
_____
_____
_____
_____
_____
_____

From Her Mother's Womb

"A mother's love for her children is like nothing else in this world. It knows no law, no pity. It dares all things and crushes down remorselessly all that stands in its path."
~Agatha Christie~

Since Monica was a child, she always kept her emotions, her problems, and any other issue bottled inside. Her mother would get so upset because she never shared anything with anyone. That's just how Monica was. She didn't see the need to pour her life out to anyone who couldn't or wouldn't understand the things that she went through. Monica wasn't fond of journaling as a child, so she never let anything out, not even on paper. She just let everything build inside until she hit her breaking points

One day, Monica's mother got so frustrated with her and took her to a therapist named Dr. Wilson. She remembered that day like it was yesterday.

She and her mother got in the car and drove 33 minutes from their home to downtown Atlanta to see the therapist. When they arrived, they were at a very tall brown building that had a dark parking lot attached to it. Her mom hit the call box and someone on the other end answered. "Dr. Wilson's Office" the lady said. Monica's mother pushed the little silver button to talk back and said "Yes, we have an appointment with Dr. Wilson". The lady on the other end of the call box buzzed us in. They got on the elevator and went all the way up to floor 22. When they reached floor 22 they got off the elevator and signed in at the front desk. They sat down and five minutes later Dr. Wilson came out to greet them. The therapist called Monica's name and she didn't respond. Her mother said, "She's right here." Dr. Wilson came over to Monica and shook her hand. Then Dr. Wilson said, "Come with me". As they walked into her office, Monica was thinking - "if I don't talk to my own family, what makes you think I'm going to sit here and talk openly to you?" Once they reached the office, she plopped down on the comfy purple couch and put her feet up. Dr. Wilson began asking the standard questions that she asks all of her clients and then she asked some personal questions about Monica's life as a child and now. She would just answer yes or no to all of the questions Dr. Wilson asked. She didn't really feel obligated to talk to this lady about her life. After her session, she thanked Dr. Wilson and walked out of the room. She went back to the lobby where her mother was waiting on her. She told her mom she was ready to go. As they waited for the elevator to arrive on the 22nd floor, her mom asked how she felt. She responded, "Like I was just quizzed about my entire life." Her mother asked her if she wanted to share what they talked about, just as she was getting ready to answer, the elevator opened. They got on the elevator and her mother told her they would talk later. On the ride home, her mother asked her, "Why don't you like talking about your problems and expressing your emotions?" She just stared at the window and said, "I'm fine." Her mother began to cry tears of pain. Knowing that her daughter was hurting and needed healing yet she couldn't do anything about it…

If you could say anything to your mother, what would you say?

Dear mom,

_____
_____
_____
_____
_____
_____
_____
_____
_____
_____
_____
_____
_____
_____
_____
_____
_____
_____
_____

Daddy's Girl

"The bond between a father and his daughter is special. The bond carries father and daughters through sunny and stormy phases, growing stronger over time. A young girl needs her father for protection. When she is grown into a woman, she often becomes his close friend and support."
~Nisha Patel~

For so long, Monica blamed her dad for her relationship issues. She felt like all of his karma was coming back around on her. When she was younger, she felt like her dad abandoned her family. Abandon may be a strong word, but at the time that's exactly how she felt. She felt like her and her brothers weren't her father's priority. She blamed him for her parent's divorce and everything that was happening to her. When he would lie to her, she was always heartbroken. She was devastated when she found out he had another daughter and she now had a little sister. She felt like she wasn't his princess anymore. She thought someone was taking her spot. She didn't want to share her daddy. After she met her little sister there was no way she couldn't love her. She was family. As she got older, she came to the realization that it wasn't that her daddy didn't love her, or that he didn't know how to be a dad – it was just that he was being the best father he knew how to be. He didn't necessarily have direct love shown to him growing up. He thought that just because he gave money and took care of some things that everything was okay. Though through her teenage years, her dad was no longer living in their home, he was still present, but he had no presence in her life. She needed her daddy to be there for her in every way possible. Once she started to see her dad change for the better and start walking in his purpose, she became open to the idea of building a better relationship with him. Monica had to learn that she first had to forgive him for all of her hidden pain growing up so that their relationship would flourish. Over the last few years they've grown closer than ever. He's like one of her best friends now. That's all she ever wanted... was to be daddy's girl!

    For a daughter, getting love from her daddy is a huge thing. How her father treats her sets the tone for so many other relationships in her life. Her father is the ultimate standard and role model for every man that comes into her life thereafter. A father is usually a daughter's first love. She looks to him for support, protection, and validation.

If you could say anything to your father, what would you say?

Dear daddy,

_____
_____
_____
_____
_____
_____
_____
_____
_____
_____
_____
_____
_____
_____
_____
_____
_____
_____
_____
_____

Her 20 SomeTHINGS

Her Gift

"A winner is someone who recognizes her God-given talents, works her tail off to develop them into skills, and uses these skills to accomplish her goals."

~Unknown~

She woke up one Saturday morning not feeling well at all. She was vomiting all over the floor, battling a headache, and feeling very light headed. She walked into the kitchen where her sister was cooking pancakes, turkey bacon, and grits for breakfast. She sat down at the breakfast table, slouched over. Her sister asked her "what's wrong with you?" She responded, "Nothing, I just don't feel well and told her the symptoms." Her sister immediately said, "hmmm, sounds like you're pregnant." Then gave her a side eye. She quickly denied it and said, "That can't be possible!" Her sister then said, "well maybe you should just go and get a pregnancy test from Walgreens." She quickly ran to throw on her sweatpants, Ugg Boots, and a shirt and rushed out the door. As she drove to the drug store, she thought to herself, "I can't be pregnant, I don't want to be pregnant, and I don't want to have to go through being sick and restricted to a certain lifestyle for nine months."

She pulled in the parking lot of Walgreens and went inside. She went straight to the aisle that had the pregnancy tests and stood there for about three minutes because she couldn't decide which one to get. She finally picked one and headed to the register. She checked out and headed back home. The whole way home she was praying the test came back negative. She DID NOT want to be pregnant.

She got back to her house and locked herself in the bathroom. just as her sister thought, she was pregnant.

Nine months flew by! Beep, Beep, Beep! The sound of the pregnancy monitor grew louder. "One, two, three breathe." "One, two, three breathe." The contractions were beginning to get closer together. This baby was coming now whether she liked it or not. She was in so much pain. An hour passed and the doctor said, "Okay, it's time to start pushing." "One, two, three push!

One, two, three push!"

When God impregnates you with a gift, there's a birthing process you must go through before that gift can be delivered. You're going to go through some obstacles and low points, but that is okay. It is preparing you. Sometimes we are not ready for the gift of purpose God has impregnated us with, but no matter if you're ready or not, you must go through the birthing process.

In order to fulfill your purpose you must A.C.T. on it.

A: Accept it- Once God reveals your purpose to you make sure you are ready to take ownership of the very thing he has called you to do.

C: Commit to it- You may have to give up some things during this process to stay the course, but make a commitment to it and do what you have to do.

T: Take action- Now you need to take action! Make sure you are grinding relentlessly with your crown still on!

How does this apply to you?

_____

_____

_____

Are you denying a gift that God is trying to get you to birth because you think you aren't "ready"?

_____

_____

_____

_____

_____

_____

_____

_____

_____

Challenge

I challenge you to face the very thing you are afraid to and A.C.T. on it!

What's Holding Her Back?

"The greater the obstacle, the more glory in overcoming it."

~Moliere~

There was a blind girl who hated herself just because she was blind. She hated everyone and everything. She was saddened by her circumstances and because she was blind she was in a state of depression. She was a student at Lumberton University in Arkansas studying Journalism. She hated going to school, because of her disability. Every day on her way home from class she would walk by this elderly woman. The elderly woman would always speak to her and she would speak back and keep going. One day the woman stopped her and started a conversation. "What's your name young lady? I see you pass by here all the time." The girl turned around and said "Faith." "What's yours?" The elderly woman said, "you can call me Mama Val." Faith was feeling pretty good this day and decided to stay and talk with Mama Val. They began to talk about everything. Mama Val asked her where she lived, what school she attended, what she was studying, about her family, what she liked to do, how long she had been visually impaired, and about her goals in life. Faith felt loved because she never had anyone take that much interest in her. Faith expressed that her only goal and purpose in life was to have her eyesight. Faith felt that if she was able to see, she could accomplish all her dreams and aspirations. Faith shared her dream of wanting to start a non-profit organization with Mama Val. She wanted an organization that would empower young women who were underprivileged and blind. She also shared her dreams of owning a creative writing studio; where she was free to write poetry and perform. She was having a bad day so she stopped and told Mama Val that if she could only see the world, she would accomplish every single one of her goals and aspirations.

One day, the hospital called Faith as she was leaving school and told her that someone had donated a pair of eyes to her, but never said whom her donor was. She was so ecstatic that she began to cry and jump for joy. Faith headed home, but instead she took a different way because she wanted to surprise Mama Val after her surgery. Faith never thought the day would come where she would no longer be visually impaired and able to see the entire world she had always wanted to see. She wanted to see the blue skies, the cloudy days, the green grass, the cars on the highway, kids playing at the playground, beautiful flowers bloom, and most importantly her family and friends. She made an appointment for surgery and went in that next day. The surgery did not hurt her much but she was in recovery for a couple of days. The first day out of the hospital, she went straight to class and could not wait to stop and see Mama Val after class. As she was walking from class, she stopped to talk to Mama Val. Faith was full of joy, laughter, and had a sense of happiness. Faith said to Mama Val, "I can see now!" Faith was shocked when she saw that Mama Val was now blind. Mama Val said to her, "does this mean you can serve in your purpose now?" Faith exclaimed, "YES! I've been doing a lot of thinking and I am ready for life!" Mama Val was excited for her and told her she wouldn't be seeing her anymore because of her new condition. She was moving to Little Rock to be with family. Mama Val said, "now that you can see the world, go accomplish everything that you ever wanted to." Before Faith left, she told Mama Val that she appreciated her being a mother figure in her life, picking her up when she felt like giving up, and helping her gain her identity and purpose.

A few months later Mama Val wrote a letter to Faith to see how she was adjusting to life, how school was going, how the creative writing studio she was working on was going, and if she was living up to her purpose. At the bottom of the letter it read: P.S:

"AND PLEASE DEAR WHATEVER YOU DO JUST TAKE CARE OF MY EYES."

Struggles, adversity, and non-favorable experiences take you through the storm and give you a second chance so that you can see you are not doing enough. Faith said that if she had a pair of eyes to see she would accomplish everything in life that she ever wanted. When she got her eyes she did just as she said. Just as Faith used her disability as an excuse to not accomplish her goals, some women are mentally holding themselves back. They are living in fear, afraid to move from stagnant areas of their life, move from dead relationships, unfulfilled goals, drama filled friendships, and dead end jobs.

There are times when we as women feel stagnant and cannot move forward because of everything that is in our past. Past relationships, experiences, shortcomings, you name it. We have to stop using our circumstances as an excuse and EXECUTE!

Complete the assessment below to get yourself back on track:

Reevaluate your inner circle- is there someone in your circle who should not be there? It is a very simple question, but very difficult to answer. On the surface, it may seem like the people who are closest to you may be great, but are they really helping you reach your full potential? If your friendships and relationships are not adding value to your life, helping you grow, or pushing you to your full potential then it is time to reevaluate. You know that saying "You're the average of the five people you hang out with the most."

When you think of relationships and friendships, you may not know, but you are greatly influenced. The relationships affect the way you think, your self-esteem, and the decisions you make.

Through the beginning of my college career, I hung around a lot of different people that served no actual purpose in my life. I was literally just going through the motions of living life day to day. Partying, smoking, drinking, and not using my time very wisely caused me not to think about my future, as I should have been doing. After my sophomore year in college, I began to distance myself from certain people that I would hang around if they brought negative energy to my life, doing the same things over again with no gain, no morals, no values, and no goals. Not that they were bad people, but they weren't headed in the direction I knew I should be going. So I reevaluated myself and began to do things on my own, until I eventually started going out to network and started building my friendships that way.

Use the area below to answer these questions.

List the five people who you surround yourself with the most.

_____
_____
_____
_____

Who are they? What do they do with their lives? How ambitious are they, how successful have they been, how happy, optimistic, and enthusiastic are they?

_____

_____

_____

_____

_____

Evaluate carefully if those people will really help you get to the next level you want to get to. Do they push you forward when you come to them with new ideas, no matter what? Or do they tell you that what you have in mind won't work? Do they inspire you?

_____

_____

_____

_____

_____

_____

Make a choice of whom in your list you want to continue spending time with. Don't be afraid if none or only 1 or 2 amongst your 5 people today meet the standard of excellence you want to set for yourself. Keep going, decrease the time you spend, and increase the amount of time you keep your eyes looking for people that you want to have as one of your 5 closest people.

_____

_____

_____

_____

_____

_____

_____

_____

_____

_____

_____

_____

_____

Be Patient- patience has a lot to do with personal growth. It is perfectly fine if you do not have your life sketched out to perfection of how you want it to go. You should be giving yourself time to work on self-development to build your character, and professional development to build a career path. Change is good and can be your gateway to success.

Every time I think of patience, I think about the saying; "patience is not the ability to wait, but how you act while you wait." When I was younger, I was the most impatient child. When I was hungry I turned into another person. I would wait to eat, but while I was waiting, I would have the worse attitude, say the meanest things, and throw temper tantrums. This is kind of the same thing you experience if you're waiting for a check in the mail, a promotion at work, or your significant other to align with you. You have to be patient in everything and not be disappointed or annoyed with the amount of time it is taking to receive what you are waiting for.

What is something in your life that you have not been being patient about?

_____
_____
_____
_____
_____

Be Selfish- Your time is one of your greatest commodities. Do not spend time doing things that are not helping you achieve your goals or making you happy. Be selfish with your space and do not allow any negative energy in your area.

_____

As women, we are nurturers and love by default. That is just how God made us. For me, it's so natural to want to help everyone that asks for help, support everything that my friends and family have going on, and spend time with people who do not necessarily deserve all of my time. It can drain you mentally and physically, especially when nothing you do is reciprocated or you begin to feel unappreciated. Once I started feeling unappreciated, I took some of my time back. As soon as I started doing that, I started to love myself a little more. I started accomplishing some of my personal goals, and had more time to do the things that made me happy.

What is something that you have been spending a lot of time on that is not helping you grow as a person, bringing happiness to your life, or is just pure negative add-ons to your life?

_____

_____

_____

_____

_____

Do Not Rush The Process- As women, we tend to fantasize and visualize how we want our life to look in the future and whom we want in it. Many of us want our life to happen our way and in our time, but life never happens that way. You should trust the process and enjoy each season of your life. The picture that you paint in your head is your plan; not God's plan.

_____

_____

I am the person that always daydreams about the perfect life I want to have. I dream about having the best relationship with God, getting a Doctorate, owning a profitable company, traveling the world, getting married, having a beautiful family, owning a beautiful home, and being wealthy in all aspects of my life. I literally get upset with myself when things do not go as planned. I tend to just look at the end goal and not the steps that I need to take that lead up to that goal. Every time I catch myself doing this, I hear my daddy's voice saying, "fall in love with the process".

How do you envision your life in the future?

_____
_____
_____
_____
_____
_____
_____
_____

Fall In Love With Your Purpose: Many women struggle with identifying what they are passionate about. Take time to discover what you are passionate about and what your purpose is in life. Everything that you do should have a purpose attached to it.

―――――――――――――――――――――――

I would beat myself up every day because I did not know what I was passionate about. All of my friends had talents, and I could not come up with anything that I was good at. Then one day I realized that I had to go deeper. I was looking at surface talents. I had to dig deeper inside of myself and realize my passion wasn't in the physical form, but inside of me. They were characteristics.

What are some things you are passionate about?

_____
_____
_____
_____
_____
_____
_____
_____
_____
_____
_____
_____
_____
_____
_____
_____
_____

Who Is She?

"The will to win, the desire to succeed, the urge to reach your full potential... these are the keys that will unlock the door to personal excellence."

~Confucius~

She is _____

She has _____

She doesn't like_____

She loves_____

She is not afraid to _____

She hurts when_____

She knows that_____

She's strong when_____

She has a gift of_____

She has learned_____

She will_____

                Who is she?

                She is…ME!

Part Two

Hello Twenties...

"Your 20's are your 'selfish' years. It's a decade to immerse you in every single thing possible. Be selfish with your time, and all the aspects of you. Experience different things, travel, explore, love a lot, love a little, and never touch the ground."

~Kyoko Escamilla~

20 TRAITS OF EXTRAORDINARY YOUNG WOMEN

1. She looks for and finds opportunities where others see nothing.

Does this apply to you? ☐ **Yes** ☐ **No**

2. She finds a lesson while others only see a problem.

Does this apply to you? ☐ **Yes** ☐ **No**

3. She is fearful like everyone else, but they are not controlled or limited by fear.

Does this apply to you? ☐ **Yes** ☐ **No**

4. She rarely complains (waste of energy). All complaining does is put the complainer in a negative and unproductive state.

Does this apply to you? ☐ **Yes** ☐ **No**

5. She is busy, productive and proactive. While most are laying on the couch, planning, over-thinking, sitting on their hands and generally going around in circles, she is out there getting the job done.

Does this apply to you? ☐ **Yes** ☐ **No**

6. She aligns herself with like-minded people. She understands the importance of being part of a team.

Does this apply to you? ☐ **Yes** ☐ **No**

7. She has clarity and certainty about what she wants (and doesn't want) for her life. She actually visualizes and plans her best reality while others are merely spectators of life.

Does this apply to you? ☐**Yes** ☐**No**

8. She is a life-long learner. She constantly works at educating herself, either formally (academically), informally (watching, listening, asking, reading, student of life) or experientially (doing, trying)… or all three.

Does this apply to you? ☐Yes   ☐No

9. She consistently does what she needs to do, irrespective of how she is feeling on a given day. She doesn't spend her life stopping and starting.

Does this apply to you? ☐Yes   ☐No

10. She deals with problems and challenges quickly and effectively; she doesn't put her head in the sand. She faces the challenge and uses them to improve herself.

Does this apply to you? ☐Yes   ☐No

11. Her desire to be exceptional means that she typically does things that most won't. She becomes exceptional by choice. We're all faced with life-shaping decisions almost daily. Extraordinary women make the decisions that most won't and don't.

Does this apply to you? ☐ Yes   ☐ No

12. While many people are pleasure junkies and avoid pain and discomfort at all costs, she understands the value and benefits of working through the tough stuff that most would avoid.

Does this apply to you? ☐ Yes   ☐ No

13. She has identified her core values (what is important to her) and she does her best to live a life, which is reflective of those values.

Does this apply to you? ☐Yes ☐No

14. She understands the importance of discipline and self-control. She is strong. She is happy to take the road less travelled.

Does this apply to you? ☐Yes ☐No

15. She has balance. While she may be financially successful, she knows that the terms money and success are not interchangeable. She understands that people who are successful on a financial level only, are not successful at all. Unfortunately we live in a society, which teaches that money equals success. Like many other things, money is a tool. It's certainly not a bad thing but ultimately; it's just another resource. Unfortunately, too many people worship it.

Does this apply to you? ☐Yes ☐ No

16. She is adaptable and embraces change, while the majority are creatures of comfort and habit. She is comfortable with, and embraces, the new and the unfamiliar.

Does this apply to you? ☐ Yes   ☐ No

17. She is happy to swim against the tide, to do what most won't. She is not a people pleaser and she doesn't need constant approval.

Does this apply to you? ☐ Yes   ☐ No

18. She sets higher standards for herself (a choice we can all make), which in turn produces greater commitment, more momentum, and a better work ethic and of course, better results.

Does this apply to you? ☐ Yes   ☐ No

19. She finishes what she starts. While so many spend their life starting things that they never finish, extraordinary women get the job done – even when the excitement and the novelty have worn off.

Does this apply to you? ☐ **Yes** ☐ **No**

20. She is a multi-dimensional, amazing, wonderful complex creature (as we all are). She realizes that not only are we physical and psychological beings, but emotional and spiritual creatures as well. She consciously works at being healthy and productive on all levels.

Does this apply to you? ☐ **Yes** ☐ **No**

Add up your score; how many YES and how many NO

YES_____ **NO**_____

Add up your yes's to see how close you are to HER. (The extraordinary young woman)

20 Things You Should Know In Your 20's

How To Find Your Purpose

The most important thing you can do in life is to find, live and share your purpose. You may not know what your purpose is right now. That's okay! Follow your passion; it will lead you to your purpose. To help find your passion, seek out experiences that allow you to use your strengths and gifts. Your passion drives you while your purpose guides you.

Through my latter years of high school and my beginning years of college I struggled with coming into who I was suppose to be. I was hanging out with the wrong people. I began smoking, drinking, and partying consistently. I had no clue what my purpose in life was. I had to make the decision to remove myself from the kind of environment I was in and isolate myself for a while so that my purpose would be revealed to me. I was so down in life because I didn't think I had any talents. I saw my girlfriends danced really well, could sing, had a musical talent, did makeup really well, or had a passion for fashion. I found out that it wasn't that I didn't have any talents; it was that my talents weren't anything that you would find in a catalogue of talents. They were just characteristic traits. I am a very giving person. I like to help people, and I like to build people up. So as I began to come into what my passion was, my purpose was then revealed to me. I started a non- profit organization called H.E.R. Foundation, where we work with young ladies with absent fathers and focus on personal development in the areas of financial literacy, education, and health/wellness. In addition, I was able to pen this book.

What/Who inspires you the most?

_____
_____
_____
_____
_____
_____
_____
_____
_____
_____
_____

What are you passionate about?

_____

_____

_____

_____

_____

_____

_____

What kind of conversations do you have with your closest friends?

_____

_____

_____

_____

_____

_____

What are you willing to struggle for?

_____
_____
_____
_____
_____
_____
_____
_____

What were some challenges, difficulties and hardships you've overcome or are in the process of overcoming? How did you do it?

_____
_____
_____
_____
_____
_____
_____

If you knew you were going to die one year from today, what would you do and how would you want to be remembered?

_____
_____
_____
_____
_____
_____
_____
_____

Finding Your Balance In Life

It is so important that we have balance in our lives. When we begin to neglect certain areas in our lives other areas suffer. You do not necessarily have to give equal attention to every area of your life, but you need to know what your priorities and goals are so that you can give the proper amount of attention to those areas.

I've always had trouble with having balance in my life, which always made me run around like a crazy woman and stress myself out. At some point in my life, I felt like I was giving too much energy to my relationship and then I began lacking balance with college, work, and my family. Those areas are not the ones that should suffer. My priorities were wrong. So, I had to self evaluate and come up with a list of my priorities and then divide my energy and time by what was most important so that I could regain balance in my life.

How do we maintain balance in our lives?

- Know how much rest, food, and exercise you need to operate at your best and execute it.
    - You must get a proper amount of rest, food intake, and exercise to stay healthy. If you do not, then eventually your body will crash.
- Get organized and create daily routines.
    - When you create a daily routine and stick to it your life becomes more organized and you now have a set schedule to achieve your priorities.
- Focus on your priorities.
    - You must come up with what your personal priorities are in life and stick to them.
- Stay connected with your family and friends.
- Establish accountability partners.
- Do something spontaneous.
- Make time for yourself.

What are your priorities in life?

_____
_____
_____
_____
_____
_____
_____
_____
_____
_____
_____
_____

Are you getting the proper amount of rest, food intake, and exercise daily? If not, what is in the way?

_____
_____
_____
_____

Use the below assessment to rate yourself on your life balance:

1. _____ my life and work/school demands often interfere with each other.

2. _____ I don't have time to exercise at least three times a week.

3. _____ I have had to give up most of my hobbies.

4. _____ I sleep less than 8 hours per night on a regular basis.

5. _____ I have frequent headaches and/or stomach aches.

6. _____ It is hard to shift my focus of attention to the issue at hand.

7. _____ I find myself worrying a lot about how I'll get everything done.

8. _____ I work more than 40 hours a week and am working on Bachelors or Masters degree.

9. _____ I don't have enough time to relax.

10. _____ I am tired all the time.

11. _____ my family and friends are routinely upset at me for not being available to them.

If you answered...

Mostly true: You're taking on too much. You need to pay attention to this, because even if you can sustain highly stressful situations for a period of time, over the long term, you could incur irreversible damage to your body.

Equally true and false: You might want to examine your commitments, responsibilities and level of control over your life. There may be one or two simple tweaks you can make to ease up on your work/life conflicts. You should consider ways to take care of yourself better to maintain your resilience and get through tough times.

Mostly false: You have a good fit for work and life demands. You take care of yourself. You are a good role model of work-life balance for others.

Create a daily routine for your Monday through Friday:

Monday:

_____
_____
_____
_____
_____
_____
_____
_____
_____
_____
_____
_____
_____
_____
_____
_____
_____
_____
_____

Tuesday:

Wednesday:

Thursday:

Friday:

Don't Live Up To Others Expectations of You, but Live Up To Your Own

Trying to live up to others expectations of you is like trying to bend steel with your bare hands. It is impossible. Having happiness and joy is not living your life according to what everyone thinks and expects of you. Sometimes, in the mean time of searching for everyone else's approval of ourselves, we end up disapproving ourselves and losing our self-respect. At some point, you have to ask yourself these questions: Why is it so important to please a world that is not even watching me? Why am I sacrificing my identity when I do not have to?

People try to make everyone else happy, but what about when it comes to yourself?

I was the QUEEN of sacrificing my beliefs, my happiness, and myself for everyone else around me. It is very draining! In my heart, I felt like I was obligated to do this. I never wanted to disappoint anyone around me. In reality I was building up disappointment towards myself. I was not focusing on what made me happy as a person or the dreams and goals I desired for my life.

"It wasn't until I stopped trying to please and live for everyone else that I began to accomplish goals, find my own identity, and become joyful."
~Zakiyrah~

Do you sometimes find yourself living up to others expectations of your self versus your own?

_____
_____
_____
_____
_____
_____

How do your personal expectations for yourself differ from what others expect from you?

_____
_____
_____
_____
_____
_____

What's the best reason you can think of to give up trying to live up to others expectations?

_____
_____
_____
_____
_____
_____
_____
_____
_____
_____
_____
_____
_____

What do you think is the real price of caring what others think?

_____
_____
_____
_____
_____

"Your needs matter too. Don't ignore them. Sometimes you have to do what's best for you and your life, not what's best for everyone else."

What does this quote mean to you and how does it apply to your life?

_____
_____
_____
_____
_____
_____
_____
_____
_____
_____
_____
_____
_____
_____
_____
_____

Spending Money Wisely

When I graduated high school, I said I was going to take a year off before going to college so that I could work full time and save some money. Most people say " don't take anytime off just go straight through. If you take time off you're more likely not to go back." My problem was not that I didn't go to school after the year; my problem was that I had not saved a penny! I could not begin to tell you what I spent all of my money on. After looking through my account I noticed I was eating out a lot and impulse shopping. Since I didn't save any money when I got to college I worked three jobs. You would have thought I would have learned about not saving money, but nope! I worked three jobs through college and still didn't save any money. By this time I had bills.

My junior year in college, when my lease was up at my apartment I made a decision to move in with my dad for a year so that I could "save money" for when I graduated college. I did better this time. I actually began saving a couple thousand dollars, but then things started coming up. I began to make other people's emergencies my own, and thinking that when things came up I always had to take care of them. Before I knew it, my savings was down. I think by now I've learned my lesson. I started learning that you don't have to put away large lump sums at a time to save. If you just put away a little every week you will be on your way to a grand savings account.

What are the things you spend your money on the most? If you need to look at your bank account, do so.

_____
_____
_____
_____
_____
_____
_____
_____
_____
_____

Have you created a monthly budget? If not, create one below.

_____
_____
_____
_____
_____
_____

Do you have a savings plan? If not, what is your savings goal?

_____
_____
_____
_____
_____
_____
_____
_____
_____

What are your financial goals for the next three years?

_____
_____
_____
_____
_____
_____
_____

I've tried this 52-week money challenge. I think it will help.

I challenge you to start THIS week.

week	Amount Deposited	Account Balance	Week	Amount Deposited	Account Balance
1	$1.00	$1.00	27	$27.00	$378.00
2	$2.00	$3.00	28	$28.00	$406.00
3	$3.00	$6.00	29	$29.00	$435.00
4	$4.00	$10.00	30	$30.00	$465.00
5	$5.00	$15.00	31	$31.00	$496.00
6	$6.00	$21.00	32	$32.00	$528.00
7	$7.00	$28.00	33	$33.00	$561.00
8	$8.00	$36.00	34	$34.00	$595.00
9	$9.00	$45.00	35	$35.00	$630.00
10	$10.00	$55.00	36	$36.00	$666.00
11	$11.00	$66.00	37	$37.00	$703.00
12	$12.00	$78.00	38	$38.00	$741.00
13	$13.00	$91.00	39	$39.00	$780.00
14	$14.00	$105.00	40	$40.00	$820.00
15	$15.00	$120.00	41	$41.00	$861.00
16	$16.00	$136.00	42	$42.00	$903.00
17	$17.00	$153.00	43	$43.00	$946.00
18	$18.00	$171.00	44	$44.00	$990.00
19	$19.00	$190.00	45	$45.00	$1,035.00
20	$20.00	$210.00	46	$46.00	$1,081.00
21	$21.00	$231.00	47	$47.00	$1,128.00
22	$22.00	$253.00	48	$48.00	$1,176.00
23	$23.00	$276.00	49	$49.00	$1,225.00
24	$24.00	$300.00	50	$50.00	$1,275.00
25	$25.00	$325.00	51	$51.00	$1,326.00
26	$26.00	$351.00	52	$52.00	$1,378.00

Her 20 SomeTHINGS

Learn New Things

In order to reach your maximum potential, you have to attempt to enhance your understanding of the world around you. You should be learning new things everyday. Learning new things keeps your mind sharp and allows you to navigate through life much easier. Start learning the things you want to learn now. You don't have to wait for the perfect time, because there is no perfect time. If you want to learn to cook, buy a recipe book and start off trying one new recipe a week. If you want to learn how to build a website, sign up for a Wordpress website class. If you want to learn how to swim, go take swimming lessons. If you want to learn how to change your oil, find someone that can teach you. All you have to do is get started. Reading different books, watching educational shows on television, and listening to different podcast will surely contribute to your learning. Start embracing new things. Once you do these things, you will be on your way to reaching your full potential.

Do you believe it is important to constantly learn new things?

_____
_____
_____
_____
_____
_____

What was the last book you read? What did you learn from it?

_____
_____
_____
_____
_____
_____

What new skillsets have you acquired within the last year?

_____
_____

What are some things would you like to learn more about or learn how to do?

_____
_____
_____
_____
_____
_____

*Challenge: Choose one thing from the list above and learn it this week.

TO DO LIST

- [ ] _____
- [ ] _____
- [ ] _____
- [ ] _____
- [ ] _____

There Is An Expiration Date on Blaming The Past.

To be completely honest, people are tired of your complaining, whining, anger, and victim mentality. People are also tired of you blaming your current behavior or circumstances on your past. The only thing standing in between you and true joy is YOU! At some point, we have to take responsibility for where we are in life now. I'm not saying you should forget about your past, but I am suggesting that you do not live there. No matter how much you think the guy who hurt you, your ex-best friend, parents, siblings, or certain circumstances deserves your anger and cruel treatment, it serves no positive purpose. It will end up hurting you more than them.

" I truly learned that the only thing you can change about your past is how you let it affect you now."
~Zakiyrah~

What situation or person from your past are you blaming for your present circumstances and why you are where you are?

_____
_____
_____
_____
_____

When you hold on to anger it just piles up. Forgiving people is better. Is there anyone that you need to forgive?

_____
_____
_____
_____
_____

Challenge

I challenge you to dig deep in your rolodex and find someone that you need to forgive. Mentally, emotionally, and spiritually forgive them. You don't have to rekindle the relationship, but if it's necessary then DO IT!

Know Your Limits

Many people don't know when they've reached their limits and need to stop. This can go for sex, alcohol, extended favors, and tasks to be completed. You need to decide what your personal limits are. If you don't want to have sex, you need to have your personal limits on what you are not willing to do. If you're going to have a few drinks, you should know how many drinks you can have before you hit one, too many. If you are constantly doing favors for people, you need to have a limit. You do not have to say yes every time someone asks you to do something. It's not humanly possible to cater to EVERY single person that asks you to do something. Taking on too many tasks can drain you out too. You need to know what you already have on your plate, and determine what you have the capacity to take on. If no one ever told you this before, listen to me…it is ok to say NO! I was always the one to say yes to everyone. I always felt like I was letting someone down if I said no. When it was all said and done, I wore myself out to the max. I was filling myself up over capacity. I was in college, working two jobs, in addition to being an RA on campus, completing an internship, and still managed to help other people with their endeavors when I was asked. I had no clue what my limits were. I appeared to be fine at the time, but as time went by I wasn't taking care of myself how I should have been. It took me a while, but I finally mastered the art of saying NO! You don't have to be rude about it, but sometimes you just have to take care of yourself before catering to someone else.

What can you tolerate and accept?

_____
_____
_____
_____
_____
_____
_____
_____
_____
_____

What makes you feel uncomfortable and stressed?

_____
_____
_____
_____
_____
_____
_____

You need boundaries in your life. What are some of your limits? (Physical, emotional, mental, spiritual, etc.)

_____
_____
_____
_____
_____
_____
_____
_____

Have you found yourself not sustaining your limits? What's changed?

_____
_____
_____
_____
_____
_____
_____
_____

Identify Your Strengths and Weaknesses

Do you remember this being the most popular question in your interviews? It never fails. The interviewer will always ask, "What are your strengths and weaknesses?" Some people can never answer this question directly. They tend to give generic answers. You need to know your strengths and weaknesses for personal and professional use. I never knew how to answer or identify this question until my first internship. I did a lot of hands on work that helped me develop as a person. One day my boss asked me if I knew what my strengths and weaknesses were and I said no. He then started naming all of this stuff he noticed I was good at and then some areas that I could use some work in. I took that and ran with it. Sometimes it's better to get another person's personal and professional opinion. They will be able to identify your weaknesses and strengths from another angle. After taking my critiques and, self-reflecting, I was able to identify my strengths and weaknesses.

What are your strengths?

_____
_____
_____
_____
_____
_____
_____
_____
_____
_____
_____
_____
_____

Questions to help you identify your strengths:

1. What is the biggest success you've ever experienced?

_____
_____
_____
_____

2. What do others consistently praise you for?

_____
_____
_____

3. What tasks make you happy?

_____
_____
_____

What are your weaknesses?

_____
_____
_____
_____
_____
_____
_____
_____
_____
_____

Questions to help you identify your weaknesses:

1. What is the biggest failure you've experienced?

_____
_____
_____
_____
_____

2. What do others consistently criticize you for?

_____
_____
_____
_____

3. What tasks do you tend to procrastinate in?

_____
_____
_____
_____
_____

Have a Set of Personal Core Values

I never thought of building a list of personal core values until I went to an Eric Thomas conference and he broke down why it is so important to have them. It changed my total perspective on life. Having a set of personal core values gives you direction in your life. They help to set your boundaries and stand firm in what you believe in. Personal core values are important to have because it helps situations become clearer when you have a "value conflict". A "value conflict" where you are challenged with something that goes against your belief or value system. If you have your personal values in line and follow them it will be hard to go against because you already know what's important to you and what you won't sacrifice.

My personal core values:

1. Being Consistent
2. Listening to God and exercising faith
3. Sacrificing wants for my needs
4. Having Integrity
5. Being productive
6. Effectively communicating
7. Reaping what I sow (Give)
8. Not compromising my values to please others.
9. Striving to be the best version of me
10. Being Accountable

How to identify your core values:

What does quality of life mean to you?

_____

_____

_____

_____

_____

_____

_____

_____

What do you value most in life?

_____

_____

_____

_____

_____

_____

_____

_____

What are your personal core values?

1.
_____

2.
_____

3.
_____

4.
_____

5.
_____

6.
_____

7.
_____

8.
_____

9.
_____

10.
_____

Traveling Is Worth The Investment

Over the last month or so, I'm sure you've invested in a gorgeous pair of shoes, a nice hand bag, or a bomb hairstyle that you've been wanting to get that you will soon forget about. You probably also have wanted to plan a trip, but said you "didn't have the money" to do it. Well, your money probably went to those popping shoes you couldn't resist, that to die for handbag you just had to have, or that hairstyle that you thought would look so good on you. The truth is, all of those things expire at some point in life, but when you travel, those memories and experiences you make will last for a lifetime.

Millennials as a whole have always talked about how bad we want to travel the world and explore different countries, but we've never done it. So, this year I set a goal for myself to travel to at least five countries before December so that I could create memories that I could hold onto forever. To date, I've been to four countries: Netherlands, France, United Arab Emirates, and Jamaica.

When was the last time you traveled. How was the experience?

List the top 5 places you want to travel in the next 5 years.

1.
_____

2.
_____

3.
_____

4.
_____

5.
_____

Challenge

I challenge you to take one of those places you wrote down and start researching it. Begin looking up flights, hotels, currency and plan your trip…Now only thing you have to do is BOOK IT!

The only thing stopping you from going is literally you. Don't let "money" be the issue, because if Beyoncé had another concert you would find a way to make sure you purchased your ticket!

Adopt Mentors and Leverage Them

Having a mentor is a great resource. Make sure you maximize it. You have to learn how to make the most out of this valuable benefit. It's important to have multiple mentors; a career mentor, personal development mentor, and then someone who has accomplished some of the things you want to accomplish. When getting a mentor make sure it is organic. You don't want it to be a formal forced relationship. You want it to grow naturally and your mentor to have a genuine care to want to help you.

Here are four ways to leverage your mentor:
- Drive the process
    - Take initiative
    - Develop meaningful agendas
    - Develop short and long term goals
- Understand your mentors needs
    - Make sure you know what is important to your mentor
    - Identify how their expertise can support your goals and share with them

- - Always ask your mentor how you can help them
- Keep your commitments
- Take responsibility
  - Identify the best way to communicate
  - Be flexible

Do you have a mentor? If so, in what areas do they help you develop?

_____

_____

_____

_____

_____

_____

List five people who you admire the most and could serve as your mentor. With each person add their area of expertise pertaining to your specific needs.

_____

_____

_____

_____

_____

*Challenge: Reach out to each person on your list and take him or her to lunch or coffee to begin building your relationships.

Build Your Muscle of Self-control

It is important for you to build a habit of self-control. Whether you want to start your own business, lose weight, save money, or get out of debt, self- control is essential. Some of the most successful people in the world have mastered the art of discipline and self-control. Self- control is about perseverance and the ability to resist temptation. You must have self-control when setting goals so that you are able to stick to them even when you come across obstacles and setbacks. Our generation is so connected to instant gratification that we get so impatient waiting for anything and it causes us to not have self-control.

3 ways to increase your self-control:
- Look at the bigger picture.
- Find an accountability partner.
- Learn how to manage stress.

Do you believe that self-control is directly tied to delayed gratification?

_____

_____

_____

What self-control would you have to exhibit in order to conquer the potential distractions to that goal?

_____

_____

_____

_____

_____

_____

_____

_____

_____

_____

_____

_____

What normally happens when you don't practice self-control? Does it push you back with goals etc.?

___
___
___
___
___
___
___
___
___
___
___
___
___
___
___
___
___
___

Believe You Can Do It

Some people constantly doubt their abilities, talents, skills, and opinions that make them who they are. The first step in being successful is believing in you. If you don't believe in yourself, it is true; no one will.

You have to understand the power of positive thinking. Let's start with believing in the potential you have. I have always discounted my ability to do things because I was scared I wouldn't do it right or mess something up. One day I literally just decided to understand the saying " if you never try then you'll never know that you can do it."

You have to overcome the obstacle of fear. To me fear is just another obstacle to get over. Once you get past the thought of fear, you'll be able to attack anything.

Challenging yourself is the biggest thing. I never thought I would be able to write and publish a book. I challenged myself and began to tackle it. It took me a little longer than most, but I did it!

*Challenge: Create a list of items that you know you are unable to do. You can start small. Make yourself a schedule and begin tackling everything on that list. You'll find out that you can do more that what you thought you could!

_____

_____

_____

_____

_____

_____

_____

_____

_____

_____

_____

_____

_____

_____

_____

_____

What does fear mean to you?

_____
_____
_____
_____
_____
_____
_____
_____
_____
_____
_____

I challenge you to ask yourself "What would I do if I wasn't afraid?"

_____
_____
_____
_____
_____

Setting and executing goals

Simply put, goals are priorities, that your aiming for and dreams that you have written down. They are the desired result that you plan and commit to achieve. If you ask most people what is their one major objective in life, they would probably give you a vague answer, such as

"I want to make a lot of money, be happy, and make a good living" and that is it. They are all wishes and not clear goals. Once you have determined what your goal is - your next step is to develop an action plan. Your goal action plan must include the following:

Goal: State the goal you hope to achieve.

Type of goal: Determine if it is personal, professional, scholastic, health-related, or financial.

Purpose of goal: State what is being accomplished by achieving the goal.

Major benefit to you: List what benefits you expect to receive once accomplishing the goal.

Benefit to others: List how others (your family, coworkers, or organization) will benefit when you accomplish the goal.

Barriers: Anticipate obstacles that may hinder you from reaching your goal.

Solution: Strategize and develop methods for overcoming obstacles.

Action milestones: Create a list of checkpoints (or smaller objectives) to aid in measuring progress toward accomplishing the goal.

Overall target date: Set a realistic date for goal to be accomplished.

"You'll never achieve your dreams if they don't become goals."

~Unknown~

What is your personal mission statement?

List your three most important goals:

1.

2.

3.

What could get in your way of accomplishing these goals?

_____

_____

_____

_____

_____

_____

How can you overcome these obstacles?

_____

_____

_____

_____

_____

_____

_____

What resources will you need to meet your goals?

_____

_____

_____

Who can help you? Make a list of people and begin reaching out.

_____
_____
_____
_____
_____

* Challenge: Get a poster board and write down all three of your goals. Put a start date and end date next to each and maybe even a picture to symbolize. Look at this every day. Studies show that when you write your goals down and look at them daily you are more likely to accomplish them.

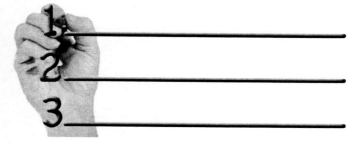

It's okay to ask for help

I was always the independent one. When I moved out of my mom's house, I hated calling to ask my parents for anything. Not because I didn't think they would give it to me, but I just wanted to do everything on my own.

When I'm going through things, I just like to deal with them on my own. I have always felt like I would be a burden to people if I troubled them with my problems. I quickly learned that I couldn't do and handle everything on my own. A lot of the issues I dealt with--I kept them to myself and they all piled up until they began to overflow. When I was eighteen I went through a depression period. I was so fed up with life and I didn't know how to deal with obstacles I was facing. I was able to hide it because my family wasn't in my immediate space. I had to come to my senses and realize that it's okay to ask for help.

"So far in my 20's I've learned that it is okay to depend on others for help. You don't have to go through things on your own."

~Zakiyrah~

What are you afraid will happen if you ask someone for help?

___

When was a time you know you should have asked someone for help, but you decided not to? What was the outcome?

___

Life isn't about things, but experiences

Online shopping for clothes, shoes, home décor, and tons of other things can be very addictive and tempting, but all of those things will at some point lose its value. However, creating experiences with that same money would be so much more rewarding. I can spend a whole day on Groupon or Living Social finding new adventures and experiences to take on! I know, a day is a bit extreme, but I get so excited when I think about the memories I'm going to create. If I could go back and trade all of those nice expensive clothes and shoes I bought in college for experiences I would. I've learned the value of experiencing new things. When the clothes and shoes don't fit anymore and the money isn't how it used to be, you will still have memories from all of the great things you got to do.

For me, a bucket list is important. I wrote down everything that I want to do or accomplish that I've never done.

Her 20 SomeTHINGS

Bucket List:

1. Learn to swim
2. Swim with dolphins
3. Indoor skydiving
4. Go skiing
5. Ride a camel
6. Honeymoon in Bora Bora
7. Climb the Eiffel Tower
8. Get over my fear of dogs
9. Ride on a private jet
10. See Kevin Hart live
11. Vacation in the Maldives
12. Meet Barack and Michelle Obama
13. Vacation in Thailand
14. Go parasailing
15. Horseback riding on the beach
16. Build a group home in Malawi
17. Become best selling author
18. Pet a tiger
19. Run a marathon
20. Go to a formal ball

What's on your bucket list?

Failure is unavoidable

As much as failure hurts, it is an important part of life. Without failure we wouldn't be able to appreciate the process. When we think about failure, we sometimes think of it negatively. Society tends to celebrate the successes rather than highlighting the epic journey towards success that is filled with trials, tribulations, setbacks, and failures because it is not so glamorous to talk about those things.

Failure is only feedback to help focus on your future. When we look at successful people, we don't realize what they had to go through in order to get where they are in life. Like a baby learning to walk, they had to crawl, get up, fall down and fail many times before they actually got the hang of walking.

36 publishers rejected Ariana Huffington of the recognizable *Huffington Post* before it was eventually accepted for publication. She never gave up. She accepted the failure and continued

trying until eventually she succeeded. Failure is unavoidable!

What does failure mean to you?

_____
_____
_____

What was the last time you failed and how did you respond?

_____
_____
_____
_____

Identify an area you are failing in? What will you do differently to succeed in this area?

_____
_____
_____
_____
_____
_____

Ask for what you want

If you never ask the question the answer will always be NO! Fear of rejection and lack of clarity around what you want are a few of the reasons why you don't ask for what you want.

3 Benefits To Asking for what you want:

1. Increase your communication skills: communicating your needs and desires assertively, provides you with the best results. You will also begin to master the art of negotiation when people say "no."
2. You have the opportunity to move through fear and insecurity. Don't let fear control you when asking for what you want.
3. There's a good chance you'll get it- asking is powerful, direct, and yields results.

What is something that you have been holding off from asking because of fear?

_____
_____
_____
_____

*Challenge: I challenge you to go and ask for the very thing that you have been fearful of asking for.

What was the response you received?

_____
_____
_____
_____
_____
_____
_____
_____
_____
_____
_____
_____
_____
_____
_____
_____
_____
_____

Extracting your networks network

Developing a powerful network happens in levels. First level is your immediate network. Grow it and nurture it. The second level is your connections network, and so on. The people in your network should be an asset, not a liability. They should be adding value; they should be able to pick you up when you feel like giving up. There are four rules to networking.

Rule 1: Give

Rule 2: Give

Rule 3: Give

Rule 4: ASK!

Give three times before you ask for anything. Networking is really about building relationships. I heard 50 cent say, "you will only get as far as the people you talk to for no reason. What I mean is if you spend your day talking to someone that doesn't have anything going on, what kind of information can they offer you? Can they help you learn something? Can they teach you anything? – No."

How are you developing your network?

___

Are you giving more than you are asking?

___

Are you consistently nurturing your network?

___

Relationships will fail, it will hurt, but you will survive

Do not think of heartbreak as misery, but think of it as a blessing in disguise. Be thankful that you found out soon enough and that you can start over again. I know it hurts, it will hurt, and you will feel like your world is crumbling down around you and your heart is in physical pain -- but you will get through it. It is ok to feel pain. You're human!

5 Important Lessons You Can Learn From A Failed Relationship:

1. You learn more about yourself and your life.
2. You learn to be a better communicator.
3. You learn the value of giving and taking.
4. You learn to be patient, calm, and resilient.
5. You learn to let go!

"I believe that everything happens for a reason. People change so that you can learn to let go, things go wrong so that you appreciate them when they're right, you believe lies so you eventually learn to trust no one but yourself, and sometimes good things fall apart so better things can fall together." ~ Marilyn Monroe~

"Things I Know Now That I Wish I Would Have Known in my 20's"

Vivica A. Fox
"Hollywood Actress"
www.vivicafox.com

"I am happy to be in my 50's, but in my 20's I wish I had more patience and peace with my inner Vivica like I have now! Have healthy and reciprocal experiences, because if you don't stand for something you will fall for anything"

Chanita Foster

Philanthropist

Director of Kandi Cares

www.chanitafoster.com

" Work works! If you do the WORK then your work will work and that will equal success."

Chinaza Duson
Founder of She Speaks Foundation
www.instagram.com/chinazaspeaks
www.shespeaksfoundation.org

"Emotions, reasoning, and logic all have their place. Had I known how to balance them when I was 20, I could have lessened the struggle at 40."

Octavia Samuels
CEO
DO Strategy Group
www.dostrategygroup.com

"Sex is best when you're in a respectful, loving, and committed relationship."

Tera Carissa Hodges
Speaker, Coach, Mentor
www.Twitter.com/Teracarissa
www.Facebook.com/SpeakTeraCarissa
www.Instagram.com/TeraCarissaHodges
www.teracarissa.com

"It's okay not to have it all together. Life is about growth, learning, and building as you go. Failure is expected. Mistakes will be made. You don't truly begin to lay the foundation of who you are until closer to 30. Everyone talks about the mid-life crisis, but there is a such thing as the quarter-life crisis. It's where you begin to look over your accomplishments, or lack thereof so far and strategize a plan for greater."

Tamara L. Dean
Founder/Author of PrayHers
www.prayhers.com
www.facebook.com/prayhers

"When you get advice from seasoned individuals don't just toss it out the window. Consider what they are saying. Learn to listen and adjust accordingly. In your 20's you are just truly learning life. YOU DON'T KNOW EVERYTHING!"

Katerina Y. Taylor
President/CEO of
DeKalb Chamber of Commerce
www.twitter.com/KatConsults
www.instagram.com/PresidentKat

"Another woman's success is not a threat to your own, so take every opportunity to support and promote other women in their endeavors."

"Every girl should have red lipstick, it's a confidence booster."

Lathyra Ranger
CEO of Chosen Beauties

www.facebook.com/LathyraRanger

www.twitter.com/chosenbeauties

www.instagram.com/chosenbeauties

www.lathraranger.com

"The presence of her beauty and purpose is not the absence of yours."

Erica Dixon

Author | TV Personality on LHHATL

www.instagram.com/msericadixon

www.msericadixon.com

"If I knew the power I possessed over my life, career, and circumstances, I would have become who I am years ago."

Theresa Wenzel

WNBA Atlanta Dream President

www.atlantadream.net

"Don't worry…that is wasted energy."

Amy Phuong

Atlanta Parks and Recreational Commissioner

www.twitter.com/amyhphuong

"No need to increase competition, just relax. There is no one directed path to success."

Maja Sly

#WETV Cutting It In The ATL | Pretty Hair

www.majasly.com

www.instagram.com/majasly

"Dream bigger because everything I thought I wanted was based on where I came from. When you have limited exposure to things, tier up fast…take more risks."

Sparkle Hyche
Author | Beauty/Style Expert
www.instagram.com/sparklethestylist
www.sparklethestylist.com
"Quit doubting yourself and be more confident. Have the balls to ask for that raise and stop doing your eyebrows like that."

Nyema Bennett

Celebrity Hairstylist

www.NyemaBennett.com

www.instagram.com/nyemabennett

"Don't ever allow any condition to change your position."

Candis Quinney
Senior Finance Manager
GE Power

"Dream big girl! Get comfortable with that dream then dream even bigger. You have the capacity to accomplish more than you can imagine, so go after it fearlessly! PS: don't sweat the small stuff along the way. Storms will come, and that's ok! I had my best runs on cloudy days."

Queen Latifah

Actress|Host

www.queenlatifah.com

www.instagram.com/queenlatifah

'You're going to be fine. It ain't that serious!'"

Oprah Winfrey
Actress| Producer| Talk show host
www.oprah.com

"When I was in my 20s, I was a lost soul. Your 20s are about finding your soul."

Drew Barrymore
Actress| Author
www.drewbarrymore.com

"I'm such a people-pleaser and from an unstable background. I translate too many things into guilt. I'm ready to let go of that."

Connect with Zakiyrah

 *@Zakiyrah*

 *@Zakiyrah*

Zakiyrah Ficklin

Want to book Zakiyrah or just chat?
info@zakiyrahficklin.com

www.zakiyrahficklin.com